21st Century Junior Library

Velociraptor

by Lucia Raatma

CHERRY LAKE PUBLISHING * ANN ARBOR, MICHIGAN

Published in the United States of America by Cherry Lake Publishing
Ann Arbor, Michigan
www.cherrylakepublishing.com

Content Adviser: Gregory M. Erickson, PhD, Dinosaur Paleontologist, Department of Biological
Science, Florida State University, Tallahassee, Florida

Reading Adviser: Marla Conn, Read with Me Now

Photo Credits: Cover and page 8, ©Jim Zuckerman/Alamy; pages 4, 10, 16, and 18, ©Ralf Juergen
Kraft/Shutterstock, Inc.; page 6, ©STT0006461/Media Bakery; page 12, ©STT0006462/Media
Bakery; page 14, ©STT0006282/Media Bakery; page 20, ©ZUMA Wire Service/Alamy

Copyright ©2013 by Cherry Lake Publishing
All rights reserved. No part of this book may be reproduced or utilized in any
form or by any means without written permission from the publisher.

LIBRARY OF CONGRESS CATALOGING-IN-PUBLICATION DATA
Raatma, Lucia.
 Velociraptor/by Lucia Raatma.
   p. cm.—(21st century junior library) (Dinosaurs)
 Includes bibliographical references and index.
 ISBN 978-1-61080-467-7 (lib. bdg.)—ISBN 978-1-61080-554-4 (e-book) —
ISBN 978-1-61080-641-1 (pbk.)
 1. Velociraptor—Juvenile literature. I. Title.
 QE862.S3R336 2013
 567.912—dc23   2012004211

Cherry Lake Publishing would like to acknowledge the work of
The Partnership for 21st Century Skills.
Please visit www.21stcenturyskills.org *for more information.*

Printed in the United States of America
Corporate Graphics Inc.
July 2012
CLFA11

CONTENTS

The *Velociraptor* was small compared to some other dinosaurs of its time.

What Was a Velociraptor?

When you think of dinosaurs, do you think of huge creatures? The *Velociraptor* was not one of those! It was a fast, fairly small dinosaur. It raced along on long, thin legs. The *Velociraptor* lived about 75 million years ago. It is now **extinct**, like all other dinosaurs.

Scientists believe Mongolia was much
warmer millions of years ago than it is now.

Velociraptor is a name that means "speedy thief." This dinosaur lived in what are now Mongolia and China. It usually lived in hot, dry areas. Its **habitat** was probably like a desert but with streams.

Look!

Find Mongolia on a map. Then research this country in books or online. What is the land like there today? What animals live there now?

Velociraptors were much shorter than
most adult humans.

What Did a *Velociraptor* Look Like?

Compared to other dinosaurs, the *Velociraptor* was small. It was about 6 to 7 feet (1.8 to 2.1 meters) long. It stood about 3 feet (0.9 m) high. It probably weighed between 15 and 30 pounds (6.8 to 13.6 kilograms). You probably weigh more than that!

One claw on each of the *Velociraptor*'s feet was
much larger than the others.

The *Velociraptor* had four clawed toes on each foot. Each hand had three clawed fingers. This dinosaur was small but fierce! The *Velociraptor*'s head was about 7 inches (17.8 centimeters) long. Its jaw was flat, and it had 60 sharp teeth. The *Velociraptor* also had a thin S-shaped neck.

Velocriaptors could not fly. But scientists believe they were related to other dinosaurs that could fly.

Scientists believe the *Velociraptor* had feathers like modern birds do. These feathers may have been very colorful. Even though it had feathers, the *Velociraptor* could not fly. Its short arms could not act like wings.

Think!

Think of some other feathered creatures that cannot fly. What do they use their feathers for?

Velociraptors might have hunted animals
much larger than themselves.

How Did a Velociraptor Live?

The *Velociraptor* was a **carnivore**. This **predator** used its claws to tear into its **prey**. One claw on each foot was bigger than the others. These extra-long claws were about 3.5 inches (8.9 cm) in length. They were sharp. In fact, they were the *Velociraptor*'s most important weapons.

A *Velociraptor* could not run quickly
for very long.

Imagine seeing a *Velociraptor* running upright on two legs! Scientists believe it could run 24 miles (39 kilometers) per hour. That is as fast as some cars may drive in your neighborhood. The *Velociraptor* ran fastest in short bursts. The dinosaur's thick tail provided balance while it ran.

Make a Guess!

The next time you are in the car, make a guess. How fast are you traveling? On a highway, you may go much faster than a *Velociraptor*. But if you are in traffic, you may go slower.

Scientists are not sure what the *Velociraptor's* feathers were for, or even what they looked like.

The *Velociraptor* may have used its feathers to attract a **mate**. It might have used them to hide from attackers. The feathers may have helped it stay warm or cool off. They might have helped shelter the dinosaur from the sun. The *Velociraptor* may also have used its feathers to protect its nest of eggs.

Create!

Go outside in your yard or to a park. Draw a picture of a bird that you see. In what ways does it look like a *Velociraptor*?

Visitors can see *Velociraptor* and
other fossils at museums.

How have we learned about *Velociraptors*? Scientists have discovered **fossils** and studied them. The first *Velociraptor* fossil was found in Mongolia in 1924. Others have been found in China. One *Velociraptor* fossil was found tangled up with another dinosaur. The two had been fighting when they died. Does hunting for fossils sound exciting to you?

Ask Questions!

Think about *Velociraptors* the next time you visit the zoo. Ask zoo workers questions about the animals that you see. Do they have features like the *Velociraptor*?

GLOSSARY

carnivore (KAHR-nuh-vor) an animal that eats meat

extinct (ek-STINGKT) describing a type of plant or animal that has completely died out

fossils (FAH-suhlz) the preserved remains of living things from thousands or millions of years ago

habitat (HAB-uh-tat) the place and natural conditions in which a plant or animal lives

mate (MATE) a male or female partner of a pair of animals

predator (PRED-uh-tur) an animal that lives by hunting other animals for food

prey (PRAY) an animal that is hunted by other animals for food

FIND OUT MORE

BOOKS

Gray, Susan Heinrichs. *Velociraptor.* Mankato, MN: The Child's World, 2010.

Rockwood, Leigh. *Velociraptor.* New York: PowerKids Press, 2012.

WEB SITES

National Geographic: Animals

http://animals.nationalgeographic. com/animals/prehistoric/ velociraptor-mongoliensis
Read about the unique features of a *Velociraptor.*

National Museum of Natural Science: Exhibition

www.nmns.edu.tw/nmns_ eng/04exhibit/permanent/ LifeScience/Age_of_Dinosaur/ dino_07.htm
Visit this site to see a Taiwan museum's exhibits of *Velociraptor* and other dinosaurs.

INDEX

ABOUT THE AUTHOR

Lucia Raatma has written dozens of books for young readers. She and her family live in the Tampa Bay area of Florida. They enjoy looking at the dinosaur fossils at the local science museum.